THE BULL AND THE BEAR

HOW STOCK MARKETS WORK

Library of Congress Cataloging-in-Publication Data

Davidson, Avelyn.
    The Bull and the bear : how stock markets work / by Avelyn Davidson.
        p. cm. -- (Shockwave)
    Includes index.
    ISBN-10: 0-531-17797-1 (lib. bdg.)
    ISBN-13: 978-0-531-17797-6 (lib. bdg.)
    ISBN-10: 0-531-15484-X (pbk.)
    ISBN-13: 978-0-531-15484-7 (pbk.)
  1. Stocks--Juvenile literature. 2. Investments--Juvenile literature.
  3. Stock exchanges--Juvenile literature. I. Title. II. Series.

    HG4661.D38 2008
    332.64--dc22

2007012223

Published in 2008 by Children's Press, an imprint of Scholastic Inc.,
557 Broadway, New York, New York 10012
www.scholastic.com

SCHOLASTIC, CHILDREN'S PRESS, and associated logos are trademarks
and/or registered trademarks of Scholastic Inc.

08 09 10 11 12 13 14 15 16 17
10 9 8 7 6 5 4 3 2 1

Printed in China through Colorcraft Ltd., Hong Kong

Author: Avelyn Davidson
Educational Consultant: Ian Morrison
Editor: Nadja Embacher
Designer: Steve Clarke
Photo Researcher: Jamshed Mistry
Illustrations by: Adrian Kinnaird (family, pp. 10–13; p. 16; boy, p. 18; pp. 20–26);
Miguel Carvajal (bull and bear, pp. 10–11); Steve Clarke (share buyers, pp. 18–19)

Photographs by: Big Stock Photo (p. 34); **Getty Images** (p. 3; pp. 8–9; curb exchange,
Wall Street, pp. 14–15; New York Stock Exchange traders, p. 17; p. 19; p. 23); **Jennifer
and Brian Lupton** (teenagers, pp. 32–33); **Photolibrary** (p. 7); **Stockxpert** (p. 13); **Tranz/
Corbis** (cover; p. 12; Helen Hanzelin, p. 15; share price listings, pp. 16–17; p. 28; *Clancy
in Wall Street* film-still, pp. 32–33)

All illustrations and other photographs © Weldon Owen Education Inc.

SHOCKWAVE
SOCIAL STUDIES

THE BULL AND THE BEAR

HOW STOCK MARKETS WORK

Avelyn Davidson

children's press®
An imprint of Scholastic Inc.
NEW YORK • TORONTO • LONDON • AUCKLAND • SYDNEY
MEXICO CITY • NEW DELHI • HONG KONG
DANBURY, CONNECTICUT

CHECK THESE OUT!

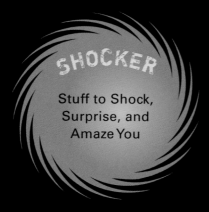

SHOCKER

Stuff to Shock,
Surprise, and
Amaze You

Quick Recaps
and Notable
Notes

Word Stunners
and Other Oddities

?

The Heads-Up
on Expert Reading

Links to More
Information

CONTENTS

economy (*ee KON uh mee*) the system in which goods and services are produced, bought, sold, and distributed

finance the management and use of money by banks, companies, and governments

invest to give or lend money to a company in the hope you will get more money back in the future

profit (*PROF it*) the amount of money left over after all the costs have been subtracted from all the money earned

stock part of a company's worth that is divided into shares and sold to public buyers

stock exchange a place or building where the trading of shares typically occurs

stock market the system of buying and selling shares of stock

For additional vocabulary, see Glossary on page 34.

The word *economy* comes from the two Greek words *oikos*, meaning "house" or "household," and *nomos*, meaning "managing." Related words include: *ecology*, *ecosystem*, and *economic*.

The New York Stock Exchange on Wall Street in New York City

The New York **Stock Exchange** (NYSE) is one of the busiest places on earth. The photo on this page shows what it looks like on the trading floor. This is where the action takes place.

What is going on in this photo? People are taking part in trading on the **stock market**. A market is any arrangement to buy and sell goods. There are markets to sell houses (the real estate market) or old furniture and clothes (flea markets). Anything that is worth money to people can be sold.

The traders in the photo are buying and selling **stock**, or **shares** in a company. When a privately owned company gets big enough, it can sell pieces of itself as shares. This raises **capital** for the company to grow.

The buyers, or shareholders, now own a part of that company. Shareholders try to buy shares at a low price. Later they resell the shares at a higher price.

Many different stock exchanges make up the overall stock market. Most countries in the world have stock exchanges. The **economy** can influence what happens on the stock markets.

Time Line of the New York Stock Exchange

1792
Buttonwood Agreement is signed by 24 brokers.

1914
NYSE is closed for 4 ½ months at the start of World War I.

1920
Bomb explodes on Wall Street. No one is arrested, although 33 die.

1929
The Great Crash occurs. Stock market loses $14 billion in value.

1963
President Kennedy is assassinated. Market closes early to avoid panic selling.

1967
Muriel Siebert becomes first woman to own a seat on NYSE.

1987
Black Monday occurs. Stock market loses $500 billion in value.

2000–2002
Dotcom bubble bursts.

2007
NYSE **merges** with Euronext, a major European stock exchange.

BULL AND BEAR MARKETS

MOM: Okay, kids. I'm off to my **share club** meeting. Don't stay up too late!

LEYLA: Good luck, Mom!

NICK: What does Mom do at those meetings, anyway?

DAD: She and her friends look for companies to put their money in. If they think a company's stock is going to gain value, they buy shares in that company.

LEYLA: How do they decide which companies to pick?

DAD: It's not easy. They watch how the stock market is doing. They try to see how a company has been performing. There's a lot of discussion about which stocks to buy.

NICK: What if they pick the wrong stocks?

DAD: Then they lose money. You have to be careful when you **invest** in the stock market.

Part of this spread appears to be a fictional conversation while the other part presents information. This makes it much more interesting. I wonder if this continues throughout the book.

Bull vs. Bear

The stock market has two major trends: bull markets and bear markets. In a bull market, there are more buyers than sellers. The value of the stock market rises. When people lose confidence in the market, its value falls. It becomes a bear market.

Did You Know?

The names for these markets are thought to come from the way each type of animal attacks its opponents. A bull tosses its horns up in the air to attack. A bear swipes down with its paws.

WIN SOME, LOSE SOME

NICK: It sounds a little like a game of Monopoly®.

DAD: Yes, I guess so. Sometimes you win; sometimes you lose.

LEYLA: My friend Todd's dad is a **stockbroker**. He says lots of people get rich in the market.

NICK: I'd like to get rich.

DAD: It takes a lot of hard work to get rich in the stock market. You have to do research. Your mom reads the business section in the newspaper every day. She watches the financial channels too.

LEYLA: And you have to get lucky too. If a stock price falls, you can lose a bunch of money.

DAD: That's why your mom is careful not to invest too much money in any one company.

Wall Street in the 1920s

Wall Street
Then and Now

Wall Street, in New York City, is the place where the world's largest financial market began. In 1792, the Buttonwood Agreement was signed by 24 stockbrokers under a buttonwood tree on Wall Street. This trade agreement is how the New York Stock Exchange began.

Wall Street
- has world's largest financial market
- is the site of the NYSE
- is named after the wall built by settlers

Wall Street today

Did You Know?

In 1653, Dutch settlers lived on Manhattan Island. They wanted to protect their settlement from attacks by the British and Native Americans. They built a 12-foot-high wall. Later, the wall was torn down. The street in its place was named Wall Street.

13

THE STOCK MARKET

NICK: It doesn't sound *that* risky. If your shares start to lose money, can't you just sell them?

DAD: Yes, but you need a stockbroker to buy and sell shares for you. Brokers don't work for free. They charge a fee for each **transaction**.

NICK: So it's better to find stocks that will earn money for a long time. It sounds like a cool system. I wonder who thought it up.

LEYLA: Todd's dad told us that the first stock exchange in Europe was set up in Belgium in 1531.

DAD: In America, the first stock exchange formed more than 200 years ago, near the end of the **American Revolution**. The Americans sold war **bonds** to fund the fighting. Today, governments sell bonds to **finance** public projects, such as bridges and roads. Buyers wait ten years or longer, then sell the bonds back with **interest**.

The American Stock Exchange

During the nineteenth century, many new factories were built. Businesses were growing. The economy was booming. By the 1900s, everybody began talking about the stock market. Many shares were considered too risky for the NYSE. They were traded on the sidewalk. This was called "curb trading." It became the American Stock Exchange.

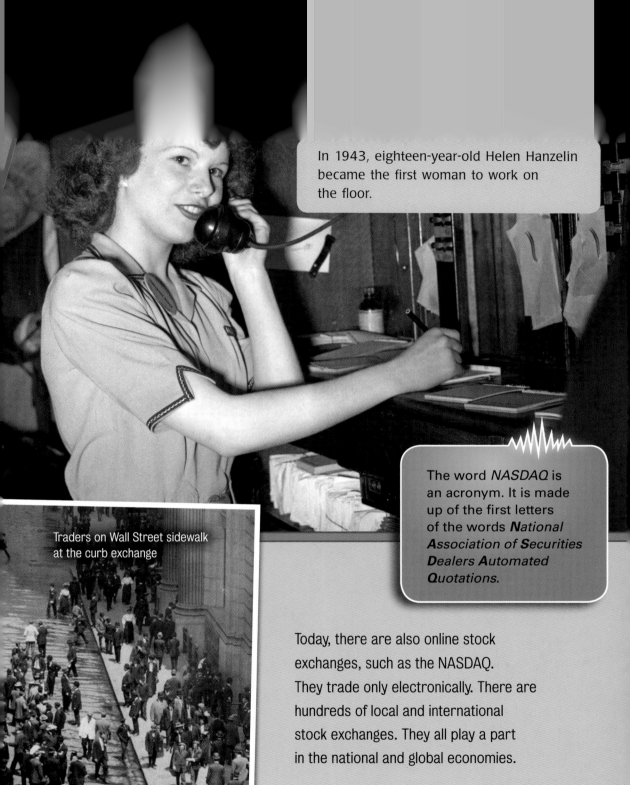

In 1943, eighteen-year-old Helen Hanzelin became the first woman to work on the floor.

Traders on Wall Street sidewalk at the curb exchange

The word *NASDAQ* is an acronym. It is made up of the first letters of the words ***N**ational **A**ssociation of **S**ecurities **D**ealers **A**utomated Quotations.*

Today, there are also online stock exchanges, such as the NASDAQ. They trade only electronically. There are hundreds of local and international stock exchanges. They all play a part in the national and global economies.

NICK: So why did the stock exchange get started in New York City?

DAD: New York was a big shipping port. Merchants traded silver for paper shares. The shares entitled the merchants to part of a ship's cargo. When the ships came into port, the merchants exchanged their shares for goods. This system eventually turned into the New York Stock Exchange on Wall Street.

LEYLA: Is that why stockbrokers, like Todd's dad, talk about Wall Street when they mean the stock market in general?

DAD: That's right. Now you don't even have to go to Wall Street anymore to buy and sell shares. Like your mom, you can use your computer. It's a lot cheaper that way.

LEYLA: Sounds like it. Todd's dad said that the **floor brokers** at the New York Stock Exchange have to pay about $50,000 each year to trade there.

The New York Stock Exchange

The New York Stock Exchange is now located at the corner of Wall Street and Broad Street. It has five rooms that are used for trading. These are called trading floors. Floor brokers buy or sell stock for investors. It is similar to an auction. It is very busy and very noisy. Some people smile. Others look glum.

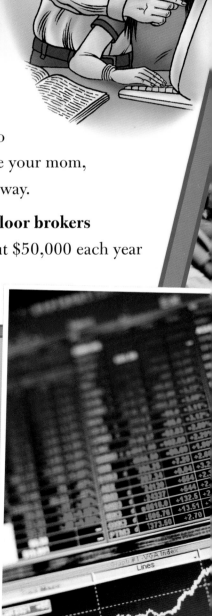

SHOCKER

Before yearly trading fees were introduced in 2006, traders had to buy a seat on the NYSE. The highest price ever paid was four million dollars!

Did You Know?

At the NYSE, the day on the trading floor is opened and closed by the ringing of a loud bell. Sometimes famous sports figures, actors, and politicians ring the bell. The last bell of the twentieth century was rung by boxing legend Muhammad Ali, on December 31, 1999.

17

BUYING SHARES

NICK: I'd like to buy some shares. I bet I could make us some money.

LEYLA: We could start our own club. We could meet when Mom goes to hers.

DAD: That's a great idea. I'll be the stockbroker, and you can be the **shareholders**. We'll use Monopoly money instead of real cash.

NICK: Let's see who can make the most money! I'll get the newspaper so that we can decide which stocks we want to buy.

LEYLA: I'll keep a record of our transactions. Maybe if we do well, we can give Mom some tips!

How Do You Buy Shares?

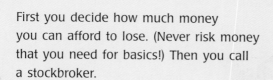

First you decide how much money you can afford to lose. (Never risk money that you need for basics!) Then you call a stockbroker.

Imagine you have $250 to spend. The stockbroker says, "The shares in Company X are worth $20 at the moment. My fee is $50. So I can buy you ten shares."

Floor brokers signal offers at the Chicago Stock Exchange. They use handheld computers to receive orders from the stockbrokers.

The stockbroker calls a floor broker at the stock exchange. The floor broker buys you ten shares and reports back to the stockbroker that your stock has been bought and recorded.

You give the stockbroker your money. Ten shares in Company X are placed in your name.

STOCK TABLES

Nick and Leyla spread out the newspaper. They read the names of all the companies. They check the prices for buying and selling shares in the companies. They each choose four companies that they think will make a **profit**. The two young investors write the "buy" price beside each company's name. They record the numbers of shares they want to buy. Then they get a calculator and figure out the cost of the shares. Then Nick and Leyla figure out what they owe their stockbroker. They deduct his **commission**.

DAD: When Mom goes to her meeting next month, we can see how you've done. You can decide whether to sell or hold on to your shares.

How to Read a Stock Table

Most daily newspapers publish a financial page reporting share prices each day.

Ticker – company symbol that moves across screen on stock tickers

Stock – company name

Stock	Ticker	Div
Radco	RAD	1.75

Nick's Choices

Caetterpuller has plans for a van for people with a physical disability. I want to drive one!

Halloween is coming, so people want to buy costumes. Walmer Smart has cheap prices.

I talk to my grandmother on the other side of the country every week. Atea and Tea is her phone company.

Tora Tola has this new soda I really like.

The stock ticker shows the company symbol at the top. An arrow indicates whether the share price has gone up △ or down ▽ and the latest change in share price.

Stock	Ticker	Industry	Buy ($/share)
American Eggs Press	AME	Consumer Finance	40
Atea and Tea	ATT	Telecoms	20
Boingong	BIG	Aerospace/Defense	90
Caetterpuller	CPL	Commercial Vehicle	2
Tora Tola	TRT	Beverages	100
X and More Boil	XMB	Natural Gas and Oil	400
Gen Rule Motors	GRM	Automobiles	600
Mitroscoff	MTS	Software	200
Makedonals	MDN	Restaurant and Bars	10
Walmer Smart	WAS	Retailer	70
Whaizzer	WHZ	Pharmaceuticals	300
Malt Tisnee	MLT	Broadcasting and Entertainment	10

Div – dividend is part of the profit some companies pay their shareholders

Daily High and Low – maximum and minimum price paid per share

Daily High	Daily Low	Chg
4.50	4.28	+0.21

Chg – change in share price from previous day

Leyla's Choices

Whaizzer develops medicines my grandfather needs for his heart disease.

Gen Rule Motors just brought out a fuel-saving car. I think it could be a hit.

Malt Tisnee is just about to release a new blockbuster.

People always want Mitroscoff's newest computer software.

Choose your own stock to follow and see how it performs in the next four stock checks.

21

WATCH THIS SPACE

The next morning, Mom comes to the table with a big grin on her face.

MOM: Those shares we bought in that fruit-juice company have gone up 20 percent since we bought them last year. We decided to sell them. We made $1,500 on that deal. Split among the three of us, that's $500 each!

DAD: Congratulations, honey! But you've got some competition in the house now. We've started our own share club too.

MOM: What fun! How much are you each going to start with?

NICK: A thousand dollars each!

MOM: Wow! You'll need to check how the Dow is doing. Here's my copy of the *Wall Street Journal.*

What Is the Dow Jones?

The Dow Jones Industrial Average (or Dow) is a set of statistics that are published in the *Wall Street Journal.* The Dow is an index of the average stock value of 30 important companies. These companies are known as "blue chip" companies. If they are doing well, the majority of the New York Stock Exchange is probably making money too. Other stock exchanges use similar averages to measure their markets. Hong Kong has the Hang Seng, London has the FTSE, and Tokyo has the Nikkei.

日比

8|
5,200
5,100
5,000
4,900
4,800
4,700
4,600
4,500

STOCK CHECK 1

Ticker	Chg
AME	+5
ATT	0
BIG	+10
CPL	-3
TRT	-1
XMB	-7
GRM	-1
MTS	-1
MDN	+4
WAS	+2
WHZ	+2
MLT	-1

UPS AND DOWNS

Over the next few weeks, Nick and Leyla watch their share prices. Most of the shares go up a little bit. Some of them stay the same. A few go down.

Nick and Leyla make charts to show how their shares are doing. They begin to search the newspapers for articles about their companies.

What Makes the Stock Market Go Up and Down?

Lots of factors affect the stock market. If a company shows a good profit, the stock price usually goes up. If a company performs badly, the price of its shares will probably drop. A disaster, such as Hurricane Katrina, can harm many companies at once. On the other hand, a new invention or discovery can cause the entire market to rise. People's emotions matter too. A negative newspaper article can cause people to lose faith in a company. If enough people try to sell their shares in that company, its stock will lose value. Gossip and rumors can have the same effect as real information.

Boingong Builds New Airplane

Malt Tisnee's New Movie Flops

American Eggs Press Profits Up

Leyla's Chart

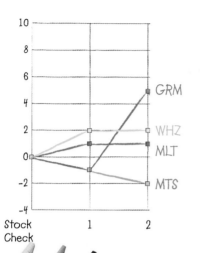

Ticker	Chg
AME	+5
ATT	0
BIG	-3
CPL	+1
TRT	+2
XMB	-1
GRM	+6
MTS	-1
MDN	+4
WAS	0
WHZ	0
MLT	0

Nick's Chart

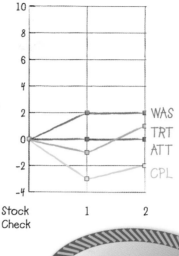

STOCK CHECK 2

SHOCKER

The NYSE was closed from September 11 until September 17, 2001 as a result of the September 11, 2001 terrorist attacks on the United States.

What Do You Think?

Some people buy only "ethical shares." They choose to avoid companies that they think cause harm. They may not invest in a company that tests its products on animals, or that produces weapons.

Water Shortage Troubles Tora Tola

Gen Rule Motors Cars Sold Out

Major Merger – Mitroscoff Eats Apples

I really liked the "What Do You Think?" section. It helped me understand how the information in the book relates to things that are important to me.

Soon it is time for Mom's next share club meeting. Leyla and Nick look at their charts with Dad.

LEYLA: Two of my companies are doing really well. But Mitroscoff's share price has dropped. And Gen Rule Motors hasn't earned me any money yet.

NICK: Three of my stocks have gone up. Only one has stayed the same.

DAD: Have you decided what you want to do next?

LEYLA: I'm going to sell the stock that's gone up, and take my profit. I'll hold on to the other shares. Maybe they'll go up too.

NICK: I'm selling only the stock that's stayed the same. It looks as if we're heading for a bull market. If I'm right about that, I'll make more money by staying in the market.

STOCK
CHECK 3
Buy or sell?

Leyla's Chart

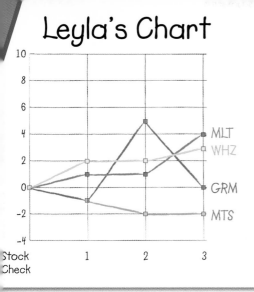

Stock Check

Nick's Chart

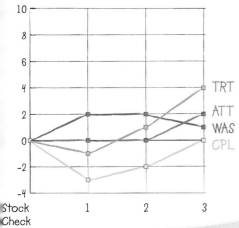

Stock Check

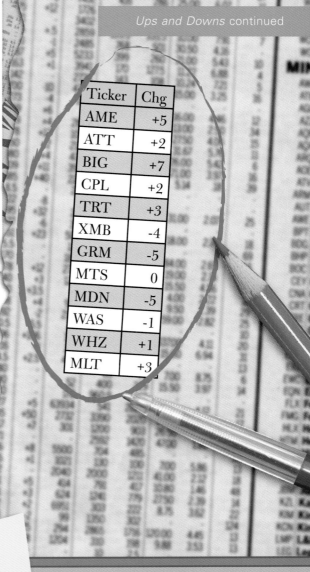

Ticker	Chg
AME	+5
ATT	+2
BIG	+7
CPL	+2
TRT	+3
XMB	-4
GRM	-5
MTS	0
MDN	-5
WAS	-1
WHZ	+1
MLT	+3

Profit and Loss

If you want to profit from buying shares, you must carefully choose the company
you wish to invest in. If a company has made a lot of profit recently, it can be
a good sign. On the other hand, a company that has been losing money might
be about to turn its fortunes around. You may be able to buy at a low price and
wait for it to go up. Of course, if the company goes out of business, you will lose
all of your money. **Stock analysts** offer advice on which companies to invest in.
They may advise you to buy, to sell, or to stay put.

27

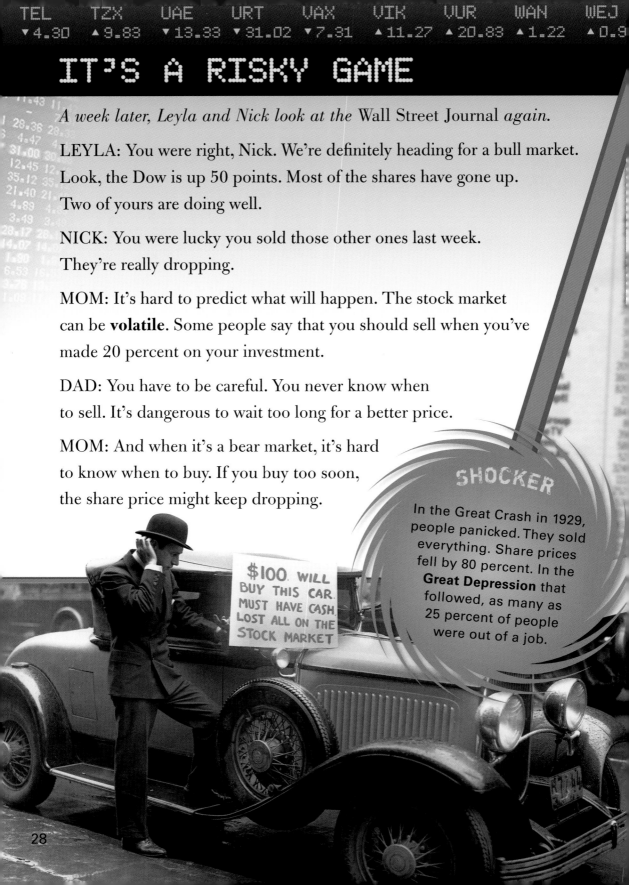

IT'S A RISKY GAME

A week later, Leyla and Nick look at the Wall Street Journal *again.*

LEYLA: You were right, Nick. We're definitely heading for a bull market. Look, the Dow is up 50 points. Most of the shares have gone up. Two of yours are doing well.

NICK: You were lucky you sold those other ones last week. They're really dropping.

MOM: It's hard to predict what will happen. The stock market can be **volatile**. Some people say that you should sell when you've made 20 percent on your investment.

DAD: You have to be careful. You never know when to sell. It's dangerous to wait too long for a better price.

MOM: And when it's a bear market, it's hard to know when to buy. If you buy too soon, the share price might keep dropping.

SHOCKER

In the Great Crash in 1929, people panicked. They sold everything. Share prices fell by 80 percent. In the **Great Depression** that followed, as many as 25 percent of people were out of a job.

$100. WILL BUY THIS CAR. MUST HAVE CASH. LOST ALL ON THE STOCK MARKET

Leyla's Chart

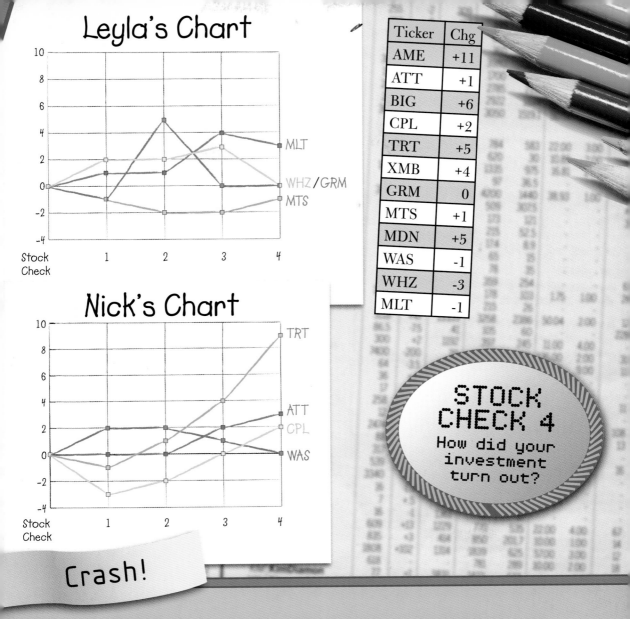

Ticker	Chg
AME	+11
ATT	+1
BIG	+6
CPL	+2
TRT	+5
XMB	+4
GRM	0
MTS	+1
MDN	+5
WAS	-1
WHZ	-3
MLT	-1

STOCK CHECK 4
How did your investment turn out?

Nick's Chart

Crash!

The stock market crash on Monday, October 19, 1987, marked the largest single-day loss in the stock market's history. Thousands of people lost huge amounts of money. Many were **bankrupted**. Since then, stock exchanges around the world have put measures in place to prevent a large-scale crash from happening again. The New York Stock Exchange stops trading for the day if the Dow drops 30 percent or more. However, a large-scale worldwide crash can never be completely ruled out.

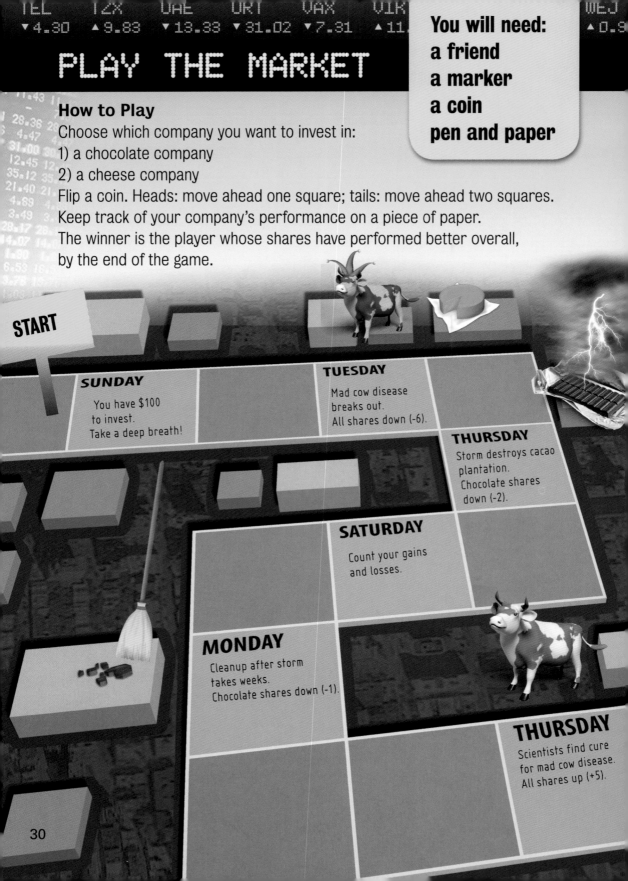

PLAY THE MARKET

You will need:
a friend
a marker
a coin
pen and paper

How to Play

Choose which company you want to invest in:

1) a chocolate company
2) a cheese company

Flip a coin. Heads: move ahead one square; tails: move ahead two squares.
Keep track of your company's performance on a piece of paper.
The winner is the player whose shares have performed better overall,
by the end of the game.

START

SUNDAY
You have $100
to invest.
Take a deep breath!

TUESDAY
Mad cow disease
breaks out.
All shares down (-6).

THURSDAY
Storm destroys cacao
plantation.
Chocolate shares
down (-2).

SATURDAY
Count your gains
and losses.

MONDAY
Cleanup after storm
takes weeks.
Chocolate shares down (-1).

THURSDAY
Scientists find cure
for mad cow disease.
All shares up (+5).

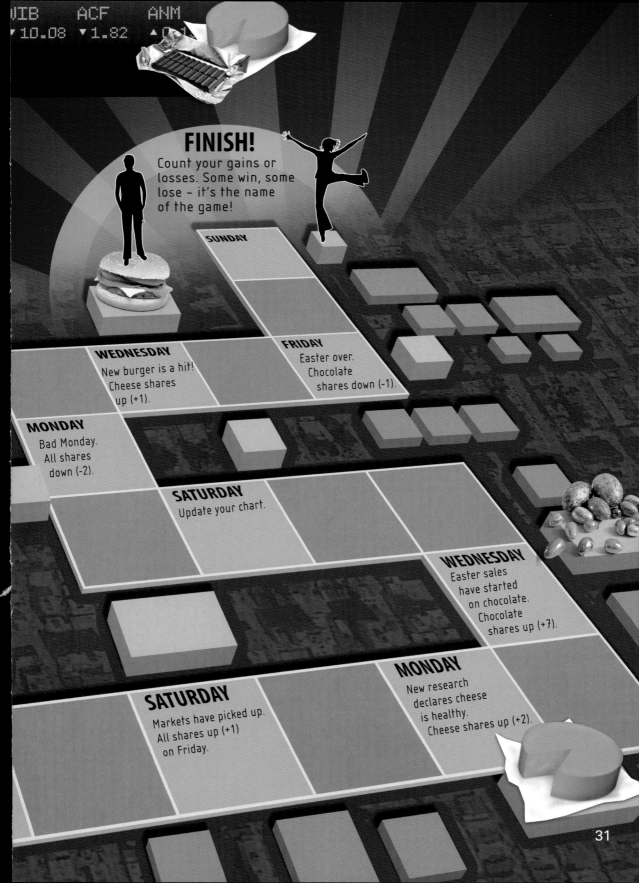

FINISH!

Count your gains or losses. Some win, some lose – it's the name of the game!

SUNDAY

WEDNESDAY
New burger is a hit! Cheese shares up (+1).

FRIDAY
Easter over. Chocolate shares down (-1).

MONDAY
Bad Monday. All shares down (-2).

SATURDAY
Update your chart.

WEDNESDAY
Easter sales have started on chocolate. Chocolate shares up (+7).

SATURDAY
Markets have picked up. All shares up (+1) on Friday.

MONDAY
New research declares cheese is healthy. Cheese shares up (+2).

People invest their money in many different ways. Some put the money they haven't spent on living expenses into a bank account, where it earns interest. Others buy things such as paintings or stamps in the hope that they will be more valuable in the future. People buy shares or bonds with the same hope for a higher **return**. Some investments are riskier than others.

WHAT DO YOU THINK?

Do you think that buying stock is a good way for a person to increase his or her wealth?

PRO

If people know what they are doing and invest only an amount they can afford to lose, I think it is a good idea. The stock market can provide people with a hobby. It is a good way to make extra money work for them.

Investing in the stock market can be risky. There's no guarantee that you will make a profit. Today, online trading is available to everyone. Many lose their money because they lack investment knowledge and experience.

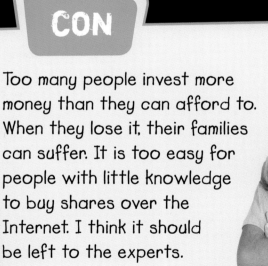

CON

Too many people invest more money than they can afford to. When they lose it, their families can suffer. It is too easy for people with little knowledge to buy shares over the Internet. I think it should be left to the experts.

GLOSSARY

American Revolution also known as the War of Independence and the Revolutionary War (April 19, 1775 – October 19, 1781)

bankrupt in a state of financial ruin; unable to pay one's debts

bond an interest-bearing agreement to lend money to a company or government for a certain amount of time

capital an amount of money used to start or expand a company

commission a fee paid to someone for a business transaction

dividend (*DIV uh dend*) a share of company profits that is given to shareholders

floor broker someone who trades on the trading floor for a client

Great Depression the worldwide collapse of business in the 1930s

interest a fee paid for borrowing money

merge to join two or more companies whose shares are available to the public

return the profit from labor, investment, or business

Floor brokers

share a unit of stock that can be sold individually; an investor can own thousands or millions of shares of a stock

share club a group of people who pool their money to make investments; also called an investment club

shareholder a person who owns shares in a company, also called a stockholder

stock analyst a person who studies the stock market and gives advice to companies

stockbroker a person who buys and sells company shares on behalf of other people

transaction an exchange of goods, services, or money

volatile (*VOL uh tuhl*) subject to sudden and unexpected changes

FIND OUT MORE

BOOKS

Blumenthal, Karen. *Six Days in October: The Stock Market Crash of 1929*. Atheneum Books, 2002.

Davidson, Avelyn. *Dollars and Sense: Economics and Science*. Scholastic Inc., 2008.

Fuller, Donna Jo. *The Stock Market*. Lerner Publishing Group, 2005.

Gilman, Laura Anne. *Economics*. Lerner Publishing Group, 2006.

Karlitz, Gail and Honig, Debbie. *Growing Money: A Complete (and Completely Updated) Investing Guide for Kids*. Price Stern Sloan, 2001.

Whitcraft, Melissa. *Wall Street*. Children's Press, 2003.

WEB SITES

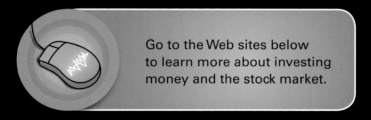

Go to the Web sites below to learn more about investing money and the stock market.

www.younginvestor.com/kids

www.themint.org/kids

http://library.thinkquest.org/3096

INDEX

ABOUT THE AUTHOR

Avelyn Davidson is the author of many fiction and nonfiction books for children. She worked as a schoolteacher for many years. In her class, she introduced her students to the workings of the stock market. Then the class formed a share club like Nick and Leyla in this book. The students bought and sold shares and read about their stocks in the newspaper. It was a fun way to learn about how the economy works without risking real money!